Fatherhood Begins Before Birth

by Chris Celio, PsyD

ISBN: 9798617987845

Available at Amazon.com in Paperback and Kindle formats.

Dedication

This book is dedicated to my children, who made me a dad and bring joy to my world daily. It's been fun trying to figure out parenting while you two are figuring out life.

This book is dedicated to my wife, who has gone through this parenting journey with me, laughed with me at my mistakes, and always believes in me to live up to my best.

This book is dedicated to my father (who showed me the way) and my brothers (one who tackled fatherhood first and the other who's the best uncle in town).

This book is dedicated to the fathers I am lucky enough to call my friends and the mothers in the mommy group who let me in their secret club. This book is also dedicated to the many, many losses endured by the bleary-eyed dads playing on the Stingers Softball Team.

This book is dedicated to all the fathers of the 21st century, especially those who have taken on fatherhood roles that blurred or obliterated the gender dichotomy of the past and found the roles that work best for them.

And many thanks to the dads and newborns featured in this book!

Other Books by the Author

These books are available worldwide on Amazon in print and digital formats. Thank you for reading Fatherhood Begins Before Birth and checking out these other books.

Oh, the Daddy You'll Be!

This unauthorized parody of Oh, the Places You'll Go! is a hilarious romp through the ups, downs, and absurdities of fatherhood

Goodbye Man Cave

This unauthorized parody of Goodnight Moon will help any man mourn the loss of his man cave as he prepares for fatherhood

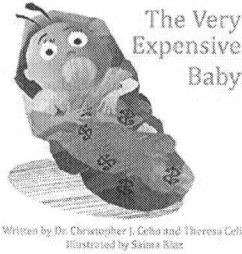

The Very Expensive Baby

Written by Dr. Christopher J. Celio and Theresa Celio
Illustrated by Saima Riaz

The Very Expensive Baby

This unauthorized parody of The Very Hungry Caterpillar will commiserate with you as you watch your bank account draining away due to parenthood

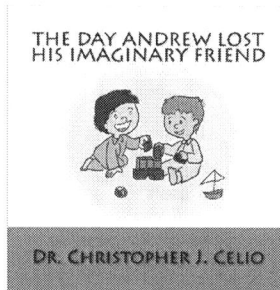

THE DAY ANDREW LOST
HIS IMAGINARY FRIEND

DR. CHRISTOPHER J. CELIO

The Day Andrew Lost His Imaginary Friend

This children's picture book is an imaginative journey for any child expecting a new sibling

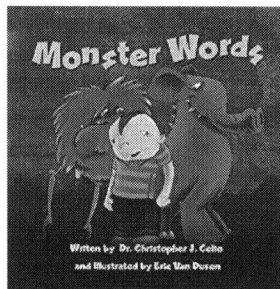

Monster Words

Written by Dr. Christopher J. Celio
and illustrated by Eric Van Dusen

Monster Words

This children's picture book illustrates the power of our words and the subtle ways we can hurt others with them

Foreword

"Fatherhood Begins Before Birth is THE BOOK I wish I had read before the birth of my first child."

~Jarrod L'Estrange
Founder of SuperDads Online & SuperFamily.com.au

Congratulations! You are about to embark on one of the most rewarding journeys of your life - fatherhood. As a devoted Dad to three young girls, my wife's first pregnancy, birth experience and our transition into parenthood stand as the most exciting yet challenging time in my life. I'm sure in years to come you'll also reflect back on the myriad of monumental lessons and heart melting moments the next few years will hold with the same hard fought wisdom and fondness.

You may have many questions right now.

How can I best support my partner through the pregnancy?

How will my lifestyle change after the birth?

How will my relationships with my partner, family and friends be altered by this new addition to our family?

Am I going to be a great Dad???

I want you to start by cementing one core belief into your psyche - a useful belief to always hold true...

There has never been a better time to be a Dad!

Why?

Because we live in an era where there is more information available for Dads than ever before. There are more opportunities for Dads to learn and gain support on how to not just survive, but THRIVE as a parent, well before their first child's birth. And Fatherhood Begins Before Birth by Dr. Chris Celio is one of them.

What you are about to discover in this book are 40 weeks of useful tips that experienced Dads like me would love to have had access to. You'll find that Chris has taken the time to fill these pages with his own hard fought lessons and subsequent wisdom he wishes to pass on to the next generation of Dads like you.

So for this, I say thank you Chris!

Because one thing I'm fully committed to providing our world is access to the education, accountability, and support Dads need to become the great role model their kids need. And this for me means giving Dads the ability to study what they didn't teach us in high school - communication, parenting, and relationship skills.

What you're about to find is that although parenting can be simple, it's not easy since we often over-complicate it because we haven't built a solid foundation. Reading this book will help you to build that solid foundation - and that's wise.

Jarrod L'Estrange has competed on the world stage as a natural bodybuilder and appeared on Australian Ninja Warrior and yet he found his greatest, most rewarding challenge was becoming the best dad he could be. He is the Founder of SuperDads Online & SuperFamily.com.au. If you would like to faceoff squarely against your own challenge to be the best dad you can be to your kids, connect with SuperDads Online on Facebook or visit his website.

Introduction

The purpose of this book is not to provide couples counseling, pregnancy advice, medical advice, at-home parenting classes, or any other type of concrete, scientific-based knowledge. I'm a psychologist, not a medical doctor, and the purpose of this book is simply to bring out the best in you. Only you know what that is and only some of the ideas in here will work for you. Don't use this book for medical knowledge; please rely on pregnancy professionals for that. I hope that I have used enough qualifiers and caveats in this book to make it clear that no scholarly research was done to write this book, no facts were checked or verified, and no children were harmed in the making of this book. Instead of science, this book doesn't take itself too seriously and is based solely on constant reflection during my entry into fatherhood about what it's like to be a new dad in the 21st century. Please feel free to send all suggestions, corrections, tips, and funny stories to the Facebook page Daddying. I wrote the book out of my own experience and so it was crafted while thinking of a man and a woman in some sort of committed relationship with a baby on the way, but my hope is that it can apply to other relationships as well who are expecting a child to come into their lives.

Table of Contents

Week 1: Stepping Up Beyond Our Societal DNA

In every movie about pregnancy, there is a scene where the man gets in trouble for not reading the pregnancy books the woman bought for him. The crucial mistake by the man was not failing to read the books after they were given to him but instead failing to go out and get his own books to read that would actually interest him. When you're told to do something, you might not be motivated to do it and you might even resent it. I imagine you've had much more success in projects that you've taken the lead on. So apply that lesson to this pregnancy: take initiative, find what interests you, and do this in your own way. Be proactive and figure out what you need during these preparatory months. While all the growing may be happening in your partner and your physical contribution to this little science experiment may be done, there can be so much more to this than we usually imagine. Why do we fall short? Society doesn't teach us that we have anything to do with pregnancy. Our upbringing, current social pressures, and most prenatal marketing all seem to agree that men will not be involved so why bother pushing them into it. So with the bar set so low, we have it easy right? I intend to show that going above those expectations can be rewarding and may even set you up to be a more involved and skillful father and partner. Each week you'll find a few thoughts and a question or tip to ponder. The chapters are just one page each and meant to be read weekly or this whole book can be read in an hour. The questions and tips are optional; just skip them if they don't interest you. I thank you for exploring how Fatherhood Begins Before Birth and taking a brave step toward going beyond what society has generally allowed for men.

Week 2: Parenthood Doesn't Erase Your Uniqueness

The two of you met, did stuff, and are now having a baby together. What brought you two together is unique. While you will find many people will give you advice on what you should do, go ahead and rely on your relationship, knowledge, and skills to guide you through this. There will be many ups and downs along the road to parenthood and afterward, so go ahead and laugh your way through the downs, take pride in the ups, and creatively find your way through this together. You won't ever know everything you feel you need to know, but you'll know it when you need to if you team up with your partner and help each other out. Think back to when you first started dating your partner. Didn't you put in time to get to know her and to find out what works and what doesn't work between you? This is a similar moment in your relationship. Responsibilities usually shift for a couple during pregnancy and especially after the baby's birth. Step up to the change, be open to it, and proactively explore what adjustments and changes you'll make.

Question: How is your relationship unique and what strengths will you each bring to parenthood?

Week 3: Rise Above "Dad Tips"

I remember distinctly the night I started writing this book. I came into this pretty nervous about birth and about how my life was going to change, so I was looking in many books for good advice. But night after night, I noticed the Dad Tips in the prenatal books I was reading were not very helpful. In all those books, I noticed a trend: they were all written for the perceived audience of women, with only a slight nod to men from time to time. As I went through more books, I found that the default is that most books are written mostly for women unless it says Dad on the cover. Even more sad though was that the few tips for dads were holding the bar very low for men. I started to wonder if there had been a man out there, reading one of those books, only doing what the tips told him to do. I imagined a man who only gave his partner a massage in week 10, took her on a nice date in week 14, told her she still looked pretty in week 18, and bought her a present in week 22, all the while thinking he was being the perfect partner. I don't know why they hold the bar so low, but I want to inspire all men to go further than those minimum expectations in two distinct ways. Besides stepping up our game to support our partner, we should also be looking at developing ourselves into a father.

Question: Are you ready for change?

Week 4: Emotional Skills

The official Week 4 of a pregnancy is usually the first possible week you'll find out you're pregnant, as many pregnancy tests work up to five or six days before the first missed period. Whenever you find out, you'll probably go through a whole range of emotions, possibly including excitement, fear, ambiguity, self-doubt, pride, and others. Whether you and your partner had been planning this or it's unexpected, the rush of emotions you may feel could be like nothing else you've ever experienced. Add that to the upbringing most men have experienced that has devalued us having, perceiving, and expressing emotions, and you might find yourself unable to express all that you are feeling to your partner. It's okay, take it slow, and let your partner know this is not your strong suit if that's the case (which she probably already knows). One easy way to start is to ask how she's feeling. Listen to what she says and explore any similar feelings you're having. Many couples wait to tell their family or friends until something like the thirteenth week of pregnancy (due to worries about miscarriage), and so you'll probably have a significant amount of time to process this exciting change in your life with just you and your partner before "going public." Growing your ability to experience and express emotions early in pregnancy will strengthen your connection and partnership and help you build the skills needed to bond emotionally with your child.

Tip: It's time to find out if you and your partner agree on when to tell your family, friends, work, and the social media world. Patience and compromise may be needed.

Week 5: Reading to Two People

Do you struggle getting those pregnancy and newborn parenting books read? Do you feel awkward talking to your partner's belly? Have you considered reading those books together in bed at night? Besides this being an easy way for you to schedule time to read them while not taking away from time you spend together, this also has at least THREE other benefits. First, since you both are reading the material together, it gives you an immediate opportunity to discuss issues, concerns, and topics that the books bring up, instead of trying to remember them after reading solo. This will most likely help boost your communication skills, which will probably help your ability to parent together. Also, it helps you get to know your partner: her fears, her values, her priorities, etc, and helps her get to know yours. Second, if you read to her at night, it may help her get to sleep more easily, which is very helpful since many pregnancy-related side effects make it difficult for her to do this at times. Third, this gives your baby a chance to hear your voice nightly. For many dads, it is hard to talk to a belly. Some get stage fright, others just feel cheesy. So reading to your partner helps you develop the beginnings of a relationship with your baby without having to try too hard. (Tip: for those dads who want to talk to their baby during pregnancy but feel embarrassed because they don't know what to say, try just telling your baby about your day. Since your partner is obviously present too, you are getting a 2 for 1).

Tip: If all this sounds ridiculous, try to think of other ways that you like better to get the same type of results.

Week 6: Nauseous Nuisance

Pregnant women seem to have a heightened sense of smell and they get morning sickness (FYI: morning sickness is a misnomer: it doesn't just happen in the morning). What do you think the combination of a heightened sense of smell plus morning sickness equals? It equals an opportunity for you to be very helpful! Talk to your partner about her symptoms, what smells really set her off, and how she is currently feeling. You might find there are very easy ways to help her out on her pregnancy journey. These may include not wearing cologne or just staying away from certain scents, not preparing certain foods around her, and preventing any other offending smells that you can.

Preparation Tip: Have you ever heard of perinatal depression? This refers to maternal depression during pregnancy and can become quite serious. The Center for Women's Mental Health states that the risk factors for this include: "personal or family history of depression, history of physical or sexual abuse, having an unplanned or unwanted pregnancy, current stressful life events, pregestational or gestational diabetes, and complications during pregnancy (e.g., preterm delivery or pregnancy loss). In addition, social factors such as low socioeconomic status, lack of social or financial support, and adolescent parenthood have also been shown to increase the risk of developing perinatal depression. However, there is no accurate screening tool for identifying women at risk of perinatal depression and who might benefit from preventive interventions." See Page 43-44 and 68-71 for related discussions.

Week 7: Being There for the Firsts

Here's something you may not know: obstetrics is the branch of medicine related to childbirth while gynecology deals with the functions and diseases specific to women and girls, especially the reproductive system. While OB-GYNs vary on when they schedule the first prenatal appointment with newly expecting parents, it usually happens before the eleventh week. This brings up a good question for men: Do I have to go to those appointments? Well, technically no. But let's focus on the benefits of going to them. First of all, many "firsts" happen at these prenatal visits: the first time the doctor checks to make sure your partner is healthy and that the pregnancy is progressing well, the first time you see an image of your child, the first time you hear your child's heartbeat, etc. It can be difficult to get the doctor's, your partner's, and your schedule to line up, but if you plan ahead, you may be able to make it work. These are major moments in the pregnancy and many men miss them. The second reason it's important for you to be there is because there are many emotional and tense moments in these appointments. For example, many women go there with a lot of fears about miscarriage, the health of the baby, and their ability to birth a child and then be a "good mother." Couple those worries with the significant amount of time it can sometimes take for the appointment to get started or for the doctor to find the baby with the ultrasound, and that leads to a good opportunity for you to team up with your partner. Lastly, it is important to attend the prenatal appointments because these are great chances to ask the nurses and doctor all your questions. You can also help out in a concrete way by taking notes on what the doctor says during the appointment as well as keeping track of what questions your partner wanted to ask. Why devalue yourself and your questions by not showing up to ask them? If you can make it to the appointments, you won't be sorry. One strategy to make this work is to find a specific time during the week that works for you and your partner and then schedule your repeat appointments in this time period way ahead of time.

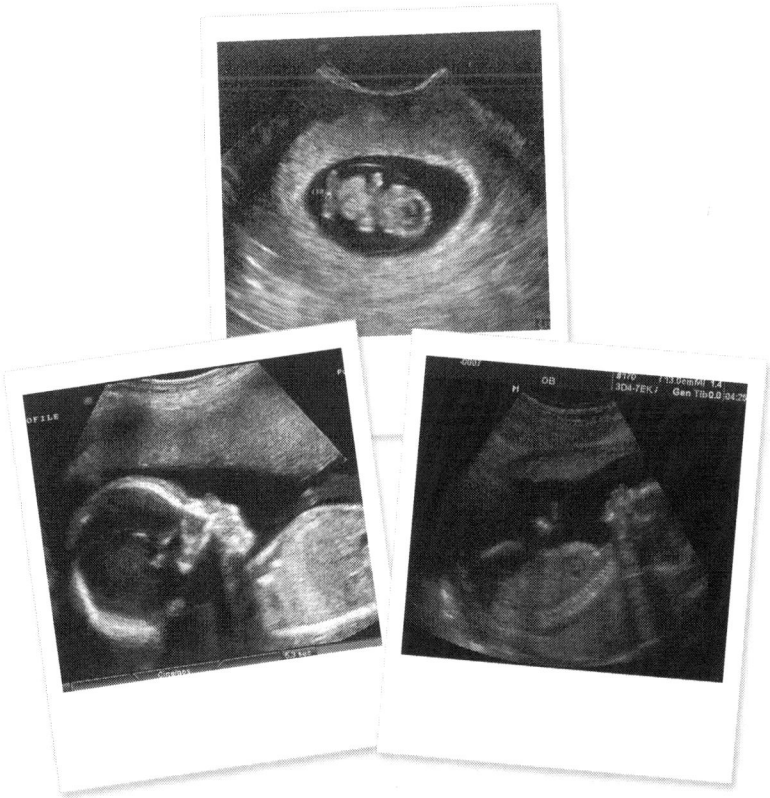

Week 8: Micro-Generational Knowledge Shifts

It used to be that pregnancy and birth were women-only experiences, no men allowed. How to be pregnant, how to give birth, and how to raise a child were passed down from mother to daughter. But now that information is available to all and it is more important than ever to be on top of the most recent advice and research. What was the right thing to do even just ten years ago may be completely wrong now. For example, in high school I learned about the episiotomy and how commonly it was used. In college, I heard how this procedure was discontinued as they found that natural tearing healed more quickly and better. Just four years later in a graduate school class, I heard that this procedure was back in style again. Then, two years later during our pregnancy, we found out it has become an option for both you and the doctor to elect to do or not to do for various reasons (so I have no idea what the common practice is these days). Another example is how to position a baby for sleep. They used to be laid on their backs, then on their stomachs, then sides, and then on their backs again. So don't feel like the most you can do to help educate your partner about the process is to get her and your mom in the same room together! You can be just as good of a source of information as anyone else. So read a few recently published books, subscribe to a few reputable blogs or podcasts, join a dads group on social media, and/or download a pregnancy app or two and join the conversation about recent trends in nutritional advice, unique birth planning, baby parenting techniques, or whatever you're passionate about.

Question: Do you feel like you can have your own opinion about pregnancy, birth, parenting, etc?

Week 9: Hormonal?

Let me help you avoid a dangerous and easy-to-fall-into pitfall: don't call your partner hormonal when she is upset. Because many men have seen exaggerated portrayals of pregnant women in the media, with raging hormones turning them into scary and unpredictable beasts, they fall into the trap of invalidating their partner's feelings by blaming her hormones. My main message here is that whether or not pregnancy hormones cause a woman to become upset more easily, that does not mean her feelings should be ignored, judged, or blamed. Generally, the emotions and message being expressed are quite valid; it might just be delivered in a way you are not used to. Stick with the content of her message, validate the feelings you hear expressed, and calmly respond. Before you get defensive, take a deep breath and empathize with how she must be feeling: her body is changing, her emotional response to situations feels different, she has the responsibility of growing the baby and trying to live up to the ideal pregnant woman espoused in most pregnancy books (eat and drink the perfect diet, gain the perfect amount of weight per week but avoid the stretch marks, get just the right amount of exercise while not being on her feet too much, drink more water than usual, etc), she has the guilt imposed by society (with society's preference for natural births, stay-at-home moms, etc), and she is called hormonal whenever she expresses a strong emotion. So, be there for her, listen to what she is really saying, and focus on that.

Question: What standards might you be putting on your partner, whether you've communicated them directly to her or not, to live up to during pregnancy?

Week 10: Join the Sacrifice

As stated in the previous chapter, there is a lot of pressure put on pregnant women. They quickly have to change their diet to accommodate the growth of the baby while fighting against the effects of nausea and food aversions. They have to learn all about the foods that have been "proven" to "maybe" be dangerous, all about the foods that they should eat daily and in what amounts, all about the nutrients they need that aren't really absorbed well unless they eat them with other foods, and all about the loads of water they must start drinking to stay hydrated. So, they have to learn a lot, change a lot, and be wary of a lot. Don't let your partner go through this alone. Be a part of the change. Eat healthier. Don't eat what she now has an aversion to in front of her. Don't stock the house with all the foods she is trying to avoid and don't judge her when she slips and eats whatever she wanted to avoid.

Question: If your partner asked you to, would you be able to give up alcohol during the pregnancy? Do you have time to pack healthy lunches for her or wash and refill her water bottle daily?

Week 11: Ease the Sacrifice

There are easy ways to help your partner eat as healthy as possible. There is a lot of pressure for today's modern pregnant woman. The pressure comes in the form of messages that convey what the "perfect pregnant woman" does, including eating a perfect diet, constantly exercising in perfectly performed pregnant poses, buying organic, etc. I've heard conversations between pregnant women describing what they are eating, only to be received with judgments about not getting enough of this or that. Bottom line is, trying to live up to being the perfect pregnant woman is hard, and while perfection is generally impossible, the pressure to be perfect is fueled by the anticipated blame a mom will receive if she does not produce a perfect baby. So, first of all, be empathic with the pressures she is going through. But the best way to be helpful is to assist in keeping the house stocked with all the right ingredients and maybe going above and beyond in fun and easy ways, like making her a daily smoothie. Or try making other tasty treats found in the pregnancy books and websites that fit within your partner's pregnancy diet plans and are not found on her aversion list. You'll be helping your partner feel healthier and your baby receive some nutritious food while taking some of the workload off of your partner.

Tip: Healthier food isn't rocket science, but it usually takes a little research and planning before going shopping.

Week 12: Silence Means You Don't Care

There is a general perception out there that you'll have to work against. The assumption that many people hold is that men do not want to be a part of a pregnancy and don't care as much about it at an emotional level. Proof of this is found at all the baby-related stores where lounge areas with big screen televisions are tuned to sports channels, basically assigning men to the role of mindless chauffeurs who need to be entertained while all the baby-related decisions are made. The very fact that you are reading this book shows that you do care and want to be the best partner you can be. But to be the best, you'll have to let your partner know how you are feeling. This follows the same logic as the saying, If a tree falls in the woods, does it make a sound? Men are not usually taught to communicate very well. But unless you communicate how much you care and what emotions you are feeling, it very well may be assumed that you don't care at all. So if this is a challenge for you, just try out the easy stuff like, "I am so excited to have this baby with you." This might sound obvious, but to your partner, it could be the best thing she hears all nine months of pregnancy.

Question: What helps you express your thoughts and emotions more easily?

Week 13: Healthy Hubbies Earn Brownie Points

One weekend, I was visiting a couple who had just had their baby three months prior. I was coming down with a cold, so out of respect for the little one, we decided to cut our visit short. My friend, when he heard how sick I was feeling, was reminded of going through pregnancy with his wife and said, "I was so worried about getting her sick, I tried so hard to stay well." The look on his wife's face was priceless. She looked as if he had just asked for her hand in marriage. It did not take me long to figure out why this meant so much to her: I've heard it said that when you are pregnant, your immune system is compromised and it is hard to fight anything off. Add that to the inability to take most medications due to fears they will harm the baby, and pregnant women find themselves with nine months of really hoping to not get sick. So my friend's wife was so touched because her husband was letting her know he understood and he cared. So, you might not read this in many books, but I imagine that taking care of yourself and staying healthy will help your partner immensely, because you'll be better able to take care of her and other responsibilities and your immune system will be healthier. Taking vitamins and eating right, getting exercise, and all the other things you normally do to keep yourself healthy are still very important. The best way to prevent food borne illness is to wash your hands regularly and anything that helps prevent her from having to go through sickness will be appreciated. No matter what, telling her why you are trying to stay healthy may score you some brownie points.

Question: What helped you succeed the last time you tried to increase a healthy habit?

Week 14: Support Style Match

So what kind of support does your partner need? Everyone is different and needs different types of support. Some may need their partner to have "blind faith," meaning that no matter what their worries are, they need a strong partner to believe unflinchingly that the baby is developing wonderfully. Others may need a supportive shoulder to cry on. Some may need someone to cry with. Others still may need a diligent researcher and scientist type. And the list goes on and on. So have this conversation with your partner, because your usual style of support might not match with what she really needs at the moment. For example, if you are giving the blind faith style of support, she might feel you are invalidating her fears (e.g., Partner, "I haven't felt the baby move as much recently," You, "Don't worry, she's fine!"). Or, if she needs to see you express your emotions and be vulnerable when she is expressing hers, and you are only offering your shoulder to cry on but not sharing your emotions, she might feel like the only one who cares about this baby. So find out what works for both of you as a couple, because this pregnancy is not the last thing you two will ever worry about. The baby will most likely provide you with many more moments of worries and so having this conversation early will be very beneficial. It will be crucial that you are flexible though, as the best type of support may vary on the situation and phase of life.

Question: Providing which type of support comes most naturally to you? Which is the hardest?

Week 15: You Count Too

Much of the focus of this book so far has been on how you can find out what your partner needs. This chapter instead will focus on helping you figure out what you may need during this pregnancy and how to express those needs. This is something that most men don't naturally think about. Many of us men have not been taught to think about our needs; instead, we focus on how to take care of others and being the protector/ provider. But take a moment to think what will help this pregnancy be the best it can possibly be for you. For example, do you need constant updates from your partner? Do you need autonomy on certain pregnancy- or baby-related decisions or projects? Do you need hints from your partner as to what roles you should take? Do you need space to figure out your emotions and time to figure out how to express how you are feeling? I bring up many of these questions because it can sometimes take men some time to think these things through or even realize they have needs to ponder. So take some time to become more aware of what your needs may be. While we want to treat our partners like princesses, that does not mean we are not part of the picture.

Tip: Take your time figuring this out, you still count after the baby is born too.

Week 16: We Count Too

In all of the excitement over the new baby coming into your life, don't forget to think about what you and your partner's needs are. You two have been a unit, a closed system, and hopefully have gotten to know how to function within that unit well. And now you two are being blessed with an addition to your duo that will change how your system will function. Take a moment to think about what is really important to you. Is Date Night, for example, really important, and even though it used to be a spontaneous event and now it means planning ahead and getting a babysitter, will you still want to continue this after the baby arrives? For that matter, do you still want to continue this during the pregnancy? To continue with the example, it is possible your partner expects this ritual to end, so talk with her, explain why it is important to you, and see if your values match up or if a compromise is needed. Don't just expect adding a third person to your system to be easy. Remember back when you were first dating and you had to adjust to being a couple? This will be an adjustment too, so be prepared, figure out what you need, and then have this conversation.

Question: What are a few really important aspects of your relationship with your partner that you really don't want to change when your baby arrives?

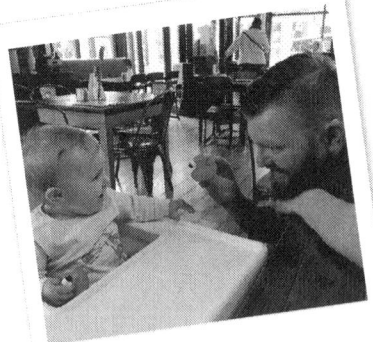

Week 17: Exercise for Three?

Exercise. To some, this word is practically a four letter word. It is challenging enough to do this regularly during stable times in life, but imagine trying to keep up an exercise routine as you are experiencing hormone, weight, appetite, psychological, role, center-of-gravity, and other changes. Now imagine trying to keep up an exercise routine with society, some books, and some friends giving you the impression that you are a bad mother or that your baby will already be obese at birth if you don't exercise enough. (Be sure to consult with your doctor about exercise during pregnancy.) The ultimate pressure of course comes from those pictures of celebrities and others looking perfect just two weeks after giving birth. What would you think about offering to exercise together? For example, make a routine out of going walking together a few times a week. While most of the pressure for the mother to exercise is for a better birth experience and a healthier baby, remember that pretty soon you'll be chasing a rug rat around the house and playground, all while hoisting a heavy diaper bag, so getting yourself in shape too will have its advantages. One interesting way to bond is to do prenatal yoga together. And don't start off thinking it will be easy!

Preparation Tip: Is it time to plan a babymoon? It will be exponentially harder and more expensive to travel once this baby comes, so check to see if your partner is feeling up to a little adventure (but...don't surprise her with a trip while pregnant).

Week 18: Rescue Mission: Cravings Edition

Let me give a quick alternative opinion to something often made fun of and complained about: pregnancy cravings. Haven't you heard, either in your own life or on television, men complaining or making jokes about midnight pickle runs or having to keep their freezer stocked with pineapple sorbet? Well, I had and so I wondered what it would be like. But it became pretty obvious, even with my first pickle run, that cravings are a wonderful opportunity for helping. With so many unknowns in pregnancy and parenting, isn't it nice to confront a situation with an easy solution? So much in pregnancy is out of our control, our realm of experience, or our ability to fix it. So enjoy cravings for what they really are: easy home runs where you get to demonstrate what a wonderful partner you are!

Preparation Tip: Have you heard the rumor to buy your crib mattress early and to set it out so the fumes can be released well before your baby is sleeping on it? Well, now you have.

Week 19: Push Gift

There's a new phenomenon in society's gift expectations that you need to be aware of: the Push Gift. Generally thought of as a nice piece of jewelry or something else elegant, it's a gift you give to your partner after she's "pushed" out the baby. Many dads, including myself, had never heard of this. Fortunately, I found out about it from other men who had had babies recently, but other dads I knew didn't know about it until it was too late. Their partners, expecting to be appreciated and celebrated for this momentous and monumental feat, became quite upset when no gift was forthcoming. So, my recommendation: buy this early and stick it somewhere safe. Maybe even hide it in your hospital bag. But don't wait till the last second, because life gets a bit more full the closer you get to the due date (the nesting instinct, an experience shared by both men and women, might keep you busy the closer you get). Personally, I wanted to surprise my wife so I gave her my push gift (a gold necklace with a little ruby set in it for the first child and a set of matching ruby earrings for the second child) the moment after we found out the gender at the 20 week ultrasound appointment. Lucky for me, my wife had never heard of a push gift nor expected one, but I enjoyed spoiling her a bit in honor of all that she was doing to grow our family. If you are at a loss for what to get her, just go in to your local jewelry shop: they'll be glad to help!

Preparation Tip: If you like my idea of giving the push gift at gender reveal, then it's time to go shopping now. Even if you're going to give it later, you'll probably still want to buy it and get it stored in your Go Bag now.

Week 20: Kickin' it with the Family

Here's a quick thought about feeling your baby kick. I've observed many men get frustrated with this, having to keep putting their hand on their partner's belly after she felt a kick but then to end up not feeling anything. Have you ever gotten frustrated by this? I found that this frustration is shared by many men. I can understand; you get all excited to feel the baby and then wait around without feeling anything. Do this emotional rollercoaster a few times and you can get a little leery about the process. Women start to feel fluttering around 16 to 20 weeks and when it first starts, it is so faint, they can barely believe that what they just felt was their baby! They get excited, as they get their first physical interaction with their child, but then doubt may creep in as they wonder if what they felt was just gas or something else. So then they go through a few weeks of this and it's an experience they can't share with you. So all those emotions flow into her desire for you to feel the baby too once the kicks become strong enough. So, my advice, remember back to when you heard her wondering whether what she just felt was the baby fluttering or just gas bubbles, and prepare yourself to go through the same wondering. For me, I loved the experience of trying to feel the kicks, as no matter if I felt a kick or not, I still felt this special electric feeling beneath my fingers as I realized that this was the closest my family could ever be at that moment.

Preparation Tip: You might find nesting and nursery set up easier later if you spend some time early in pregnancy giving away stuff you don't really need around your house. This is especially true if you are converting a man cave or office to the nursery. You'll be adding a lot of new clothes, equipment, diapers, etc to your life so getting rid of clutter can help keep life simpler. (See below for a page from my fun little parody, Goodbye Man Cave, on Amazon for an illustrated example of this. It makes an excellent gift to welcome other new dads into the club of fatherhood)

(This page from **Goodbye Man Cave** shows the drastic change from man cave to nursery)

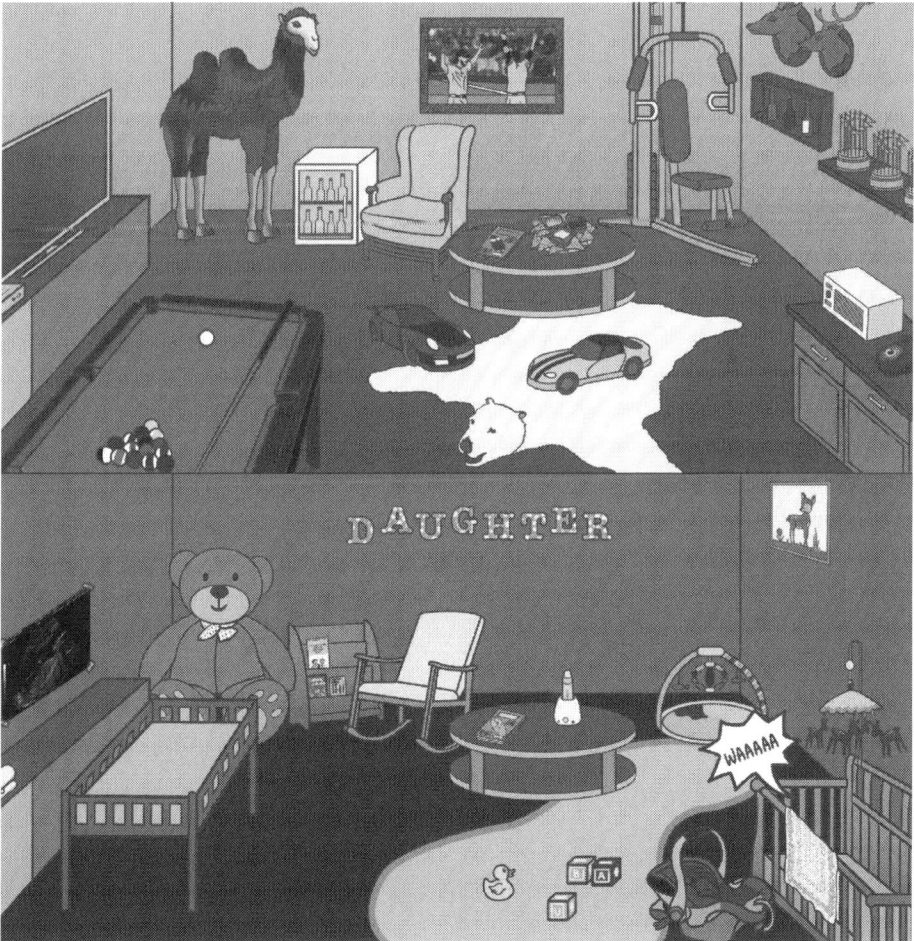

Week 21: That's My Boy? Daddy's Little Girl?

What are your thoughts on gender? Are you looking for a boy to carry on the family name and play football with? Or are you hoping for a Daddy's Little Girl to spoil, protect, and walk down the aisle? Since this is your first child, it can be hard to avoid stereotypes like these as you try to imagine who your child will grow up to be. Remember though that in today's world, your child will get to grow up to be whatever they want to be, and isn't that exciting? Do you feel like you'll be just as excited for either gender, as long as your baby is healthy? Do you worry you and your partner will be rooting for opposite genders? Is your preference a really strong desire or just a mild hope? If you have a strong desire for either gender, what do you think is behind it? Do you fear you won't know how to parent a daughter? Do you fear a boy would turn out just like you? Or do you want to create the "perfect family," with a certain gender being the first born? Whatever the reason, have you talked to your partner about your preference? It's quite reasonable to expect her to have similar fears or hopes and you might even have the same ones. You might want to think about this before talking about it. Remember, as I've said before, we all get socialized as we grow up and we absorb many of society's attitudes, fears, and assumptions. If you're like many men, and you're hoping for a boy, is this because that is what you want or because that is what you've been socialized to hope for? Or maybe it is simply because you're a guy, and you were a boy, and you think you know boy stuff better. Whatever the reason, it probably makes sense, just make sure you listen to your partner and her hopes and preference. Of course, I've always felt parents rooting for a certain gender are getting an early education about how little we as parents can be in control.

Preparation Tip: Have you seen any of the gender reveal ideas on the internet? There are so many great videos of when these worked and also great videos of fails. Check them out to see if you want to do it. Beware though, there are several videos proving that it doesn't always go the way you plan. Don't be that dad that swings a bat (to hit a ball that explodes in either a cloud of pink or blue dust) and hits his partner!

boy or girl?

Week 22: Baby Clothes Cheat Sheet

Buying baby clothes is not easy. This is a secret science, with the knowledge of this illogical math usually passed down from mother to daughter, skipping over any male generations. I compare baby clothes shopping to the difference between men and women's clothes. Men's pants are sized by waist and leg lengths in inches. Very simple, anyone with a tape measure can figure out their size. Now imagine a man going to the store to buy a pair of pants for his partner. He could have even secretly measured her waist and would still fail. What is a size 0 anyways? In men's sizes, it means you've been cremated. So the man buys flowers instead to apologize for coming home without her pants. Don't let this happen to you when shopping for your child. Baby clothes are all sized by months, but you can't just compare them to your child's age. If you did this, your child would be wearing some tight clothes, because usually the clothes are meant to be worn up until that age. For example, something that is size 3-months is usually worn up until 3 months and is slightly larger than 0-3 months clothes. The confusion is multiplied when you are trying to buy clothes for the future and you have to figure out what size she'll be at a certain point in the future. In this equation, you have to keep in mind your baby's age, the size differential, and what season it will be. And here is where we get laughed at the most. Coming home with an Easter dress that she'll fit it in from October to December or with a beautiful warm winter onesie that she'll fit it in the extreme heat of summer are sure ways of getting yourself sent back to the store. Instead of guessing, try using the table in Appendix IV on the last pages of this book to determine which season you'll be in for each size. I imagine in some areas the winter season would stretch on longer. Plus, babies all grow differently, and if it's a large or small baby, the table could be a bit off. With your new knowledge, answer the following question: If my baby is 4 months old in January and I want to buy her a dress for the holidays, then the size I need is: A) Newborn, B) 18 Months, C) 1T, or D) Call the Wife. While D is a great answer, you no longer have to do that, B is right, C doesn't exist, and A represents all the clothes you spent hundreds on that you just packed away in your garage or gave to a neighbor after being worn once each, if that.

(**The Very Expensive Baby** depicts the cost of a growing baby)

Week 23: Dreams Are Born

What are your dreams and goals, now that you have this child entering your life? Are they changing? Now that you are going to be a parent, are dreams of coaching soccer, leading scouts, teaching your little one how to ride a bike, hosting sleepovers, joining the PTA, passing down knowledge, and other dreams starting to come into focus for you? What kind of parent do you want to be? Do you think you'll be the disciplinarian, the pushover, the educator, the scheduler, the carpooler, the spoiler, and/or the sports guru? Will you and your partner be equal partners in everything? Will you each take care of different aspects of the household and parenting? The nice thing about having a child is that you have a chance to redefine who you are and who you want to be. No matter who you were, this child will only know you starting from their birthday on. So, while it might be very easy to slip into the good and bad patterns of ourselves or those before us, take a moment to figure who you want to be with your child and how you will accomplish that. Then, choicefully go and develop into that parent, adjusting as you go to the realities of your unique child.

Preparation Tip: Will you be painting your nursery? Pro-Tip: buying no-VOC paint will probably make your partner happy by keeping the amount of fumes and paint smell down in your house.

Psychology Tip: Remember that your dreams for your child will need to leave room for their own dreams to take over as they grow up.

Week 24: We're Expecting...Changes

What life changes are you expecting with the birth of this child? Have you thought this through? Don't wait for your partner to tell you what changes you'll have to make; take some time and think about your routines, hobbies, and work. What will have to change, what do you want to change, and what do you not really want to change? There will definitely be adjustments to your life. The more active you are in figuring out what adjustments need to be made, the more happy you're likely to be with what those are. An example that I can give was changing from watching football games live to recording them on my DVR and watching them at whatever time and speed life allows. DVR'ing meant I never had to get upset about missing something and it was an easy change to make regarding one of my favorite pastimes (plus using the 30 second fast forward button between plays meant I got to see all the plays in half the time).

Preparation Tip: Are you invited to the Baby Shower? These days, sometimes you are. I prefer my family's tradition of a Baby Bowl, where we men go play sports in honor of the dad-to-be while the ladies do the Baby Shower. I know, I spend so much time talking about how men can be more involved in the events of the pregnancy, but it doesn't mean we have to do everything together or give up activities that we love.

Week 25: Daddy Time

Now is a great time for you to think about what special rituals you want to have with your baby. Let me give a personal example to highlight this. My wife had read about the suggestion to have the dad have a special feeding that he does daily, even when mom is home. So during her maternity leave, when she was available 24/7 to feed our baby, she still pumped and had a bottle ready for me. I really enjoyed this ritual and it helped me feel confident when my wife wasn't home. Take a moment to think about if there is anything you want to be special to you and your baby. Another example is that some men make bath time their special time with their baby. I imagine that most of the time you'll switch off most duties or do whatever makes sense that day at that time, but do a self-check for something you want to be honored as time for just you and your child.

Preparation Tip: Is it time to upgrade your two-seat sports car or motorcycle to a family car or van? Might as well take care of this earlier instead of later.

(This page from **Monster Words** celebrates a father's love)

Week 26: Couvade Cravings?

Have you heard of couvades symptoms? These are pregnancy symptoms that men experience. Will you experience them? Who knows, but if you do, take them as nature's way to help you empathize with your partner. Whether it is increased hunger, back pains, nausea, or something else, take a moment to appreciate all that your partner is experiencing during this nine-month journey but don't let yourself be grounded from duty due to one tenth of the symptoms she's experiencing. If you do, you'll be supporting the man-cold stereotype.

Preparation Tip: If you are doing cloth diapers, you'll want to cash out your 401k to buy diapers, a diaper can, washable liners, and install the sprayer early.

(This page from **The Very Expensive Baby** celebrates how parents reaffirm their love for their child one bill at a time)

She started to drain their bank accounts.

Week 27: Natural vs. Medically Unassisted

The birth plan. Do you feel a part of it? Some men stay out of these decisions all together, never wanting to dictate to their partner what they will go through with their body. Other men are highly opinionated about the subject, wanting only a (fill in the blank) type of birth. While these choices will affect your partner a whole lot more than they will you (that just might be an understatement), you should still respectfully communicate to your partner what is important to you. Do you want your baby to be born without your partner using pain medications (this might be a hard sell)? Do you want your partner to use all comfort-inducing options (to some women, this might also be a hard sell)? If you feel strongly, voice your opinion early because otherwise you'll be left out of the decision. Remember though that it is your partner's body and so these decisions are ultimately hers.

Personally, I do not believe that the terms natural versus unnatural births should be used to describe whether or not pain medications are used or not. A professor of mine once said, "If a woman wants to have a natural birth, she should go out in a field and squat." I believe that using the term natural puts unneeded stress on women to go through one of life's most painful (I'm told) experiences without any relief. A huge majority of women use pain medication yet a huge majority of women are made to feel guilty. If I was going to give birth, I'd be signing up for medication for sure!

Preparation Tip: Do you have pets, lawns, or other responsibilities you'll need assistance with while you're at the hospital for a few days? Time to recruit some help!

Week 28: Nesting and Nursery Rooms

Nesting can be a stressful experience on the relationship. It may be the first time you two have had to debate if that dusty, hairy, lifesize Chewbacca doll should be kept or donated. To her, it may be a nuisance she tolerated until now when she feels it's obviously a baby hazard that could rain wookie on a crawling baby. To you, it might represent an emotional tie to your childhood and all that you hope to pass down to your baby. If the two of you can't agree on keeping or getting rid of something, try to figure out what the fight is really about. For example, she might have less concern about the thing you want to keep than wondering whether your priorities are changing toward becoming a family or not. Probably expressing your feelings could help the conversation end well for you.

Question: Will you take an active role in the planning of the nursery? A lot of men feel that their only way to impact the nursery is by doing the physical practical tasks, like building the crib and putting up chair-moulding. But I might mention that there are so many other ways to take an active role in the nursery design and creation. For example, nursery accessories are now a big business and there are a ton of choices. Talk about what you both want and combine both of your tastes and talents to create the perfect nursery. If you don't take an active role in the creation of the nursery, then that might set up a precedent for that to be a room in which you don't get a say or feel comfortable or confident later.

Week 29: Stress vs. Stress

This is a great time to think about how each of you responds to stress. Maybe finding out you were pregnant was stressful. Or maybe trying to figure out how you'll afford to have this baby or raise this child has been stressful. Or maybe you find many of the choices, purchases, or classes stressful. How did you respond to that stress? Was your partner stressed about the same issues or different ones? How did she respond to stress? What happened to your relationship when one or both of you were stressed? What was that like, how long did it last, and what happened to bring you both back into balance? What could one or both of you have done differently? Some of these are hard questions, some you may never really get a handle on, but trying to answer them now will be very helpful for your relationship as you approach the biggest demand on your relationship's teamwork you've probably faced so far.

After the baby comes, look out for stress triggers like lack of sleep or the effects of constantly interrupted sleep, balancing work and this new life, a baby that is hard to soothe or get to sleep, a baby with a disability or special needs, a baby with reflux or eczema, divergent ideas of what to do (e.g. to get your child to sleep, to help them heal, to soothe them, etc), two battling sets of advice from in-laws, or two battling sets of demands or customs from both sides of the family.

Since you're reading this book and preparing emotionally for this child within yourself and with your partner, you'll have a head start on dealing with each stressor as they come. But because you'll be at your worst (lack of sleep, a dizzying amount of change all one time, confronting brand new challenges daily, etc), you may not be able to recognize the cause of these stresses in the moment. If you find yourself spiraling out of control, find some time to relax and get some perspective on the current stressor and what the underlying causes might be.

Preparation Tip: Postpartum Depression is literally a killer and does not get talked about enough. Please talk to your partner a little about it and do be on the look out for these warning signs, as copied from the Mayo Clinic:

Depressed mood or severe mood swings, excessive crying, difficulty bonding with your baby, withdrawing from family and friends, loss of appetite or eating much more than usual, inability to sleep or sleeping too much, overwhelming fatigue or loss of energy, reduced interest and pleasure in activities you used to enjoy, intense irritability and anger, fear that you're not a good mother, feelings of worthlessness, shame, guilt or inadequacy, diminished ability to think clearly, concentrate or make decisions, severe anxiety and panic attacks, thoughts of harming yourself or your baby, and/or recurrent thoughts of death or suicide.

Let her know that if she's feeling a little like this, she can talk to you and that you'll be there for her, you won't judge her, you will be ready to help in any way she asks, and that you won't try to change her or dismiss her feelings. Let her know that it's okay if maybe she is not ready to tell you about these feelings but that she could talk to her mom or your mom, to a therapist or other professional, to a religious advisor, or to other friends and family. The main point is that you should help her feel comfortable talking to you or others when these feelings start to creep up, because the dangerous and insidious nature of these feelings is that they feel completely natural. What I mean is that usually people think they'll know they are having postpartum because they think the feelings will feel external, alien, or not normal. But the symptoms actually feel like your true feelings and so they can be hard to catch as postpartum depression. So with you watching out for symptoms and your partner feeling comfortable talking to you or someone else, then you'll have the start of a good game plan to help her through if she does experience this.

Your homework is to look up more about this and the less severe form called Postpartum Baby Blues and the worse form called Postpartum Psychosis. Just talking about this could save the lives of people you love.

(This page from **Oh, the Daddy You'll Be!** shows the healing power of talking openly and hanging out with other parents)

And when you're not good, there's a very good chance
you'll meet lots of others wearing the same pants.
There are many here, in the place between perfect and you,
that can prove perfect's so far
from what parents can do.

Week 30: Nobody Puts Baby-Momma in the Corner

This is just a quick warning about one very common issue I hear from mothers of newborns. When your baby is born, be sure to pay attention to your partner as well as your baby. This moment is going to be at the top of your list of best experiences in your life, and of course you want to get to know this new little one in your life ASAP, and you have been waiting nine months to interact with your baby, and you'll want to show everyone what a proud papa you are; but, be sure to show your partner and everyone in the room how proud you are of the mother of your child. Give her some attention, love, and credit for what she just went through but also make sure she gets the space she needs to recover after what she just went through. While saying how amazing your little one is, make sure to say how amazing your partner is for carrying and delivering that little one. When family rushes into the hospital room to see the baby, make sure you navigate people toward your partner as well (if she's feeling up to it).

Preparation Tip: Talk with your partner about how much time you and her will want with the baby before you let family and friends visit. Make sure to let everyone know what this timeframe will be so that they can prepare themselves to follow your request. We told our family they would know immediately when the baby was born but that we would want the first hour to ourselves (for special bonding time and to support the beginning of breast feeding). You may also want to let them know if you want radio silence on social media regarding the birth if you want to make the announcement yourself. A lot of well-meaning, excited family members could spoil this moment for you if you don't set down expectations.

Week 31: Work After Birth

Have you and your partner discussed how long you'll each take for maternity and paternity leave? Or how you'll each rearrange or cut back work schedules? These are important topics to discuss early, as it might take time with either your or her job to request and then confirm the requests you'll need to raise your baby. Please remember that society has awarded you certain privileges that you should not take for granted or pretend do not exist. As a man, you are magically awarded the assumption that your partner will do all the changing with her work schedule, or that she'll stay home with your baby, or that she'll arrange for daycare. So take a moment to think about this. Have you ever considered being the one staying home with the baby? Or reducing your hours instead of reducing hers? Or you being the one to drop off and pick up at daycare? It's okay if you haven't, and even if it's a ridiculous topic to ponder because you might make way more money than she does or if your job has much better benefits, just take a moment to think it over and let her know you did. You might find that she laughs along with you for even considering this, or you may find that she really appreciates you pondering these questions in a more egalitarian manner. And for some of you, the answer to these questions might be that you are the one who makes more of an adjustment or stays home fully, which I think you'll enjoy. More and more dads are staying home full or part time, so if you do this too, you'll have a community of dads to hang with if you prefer.

Preparation Tip: Many forms of baby proofing are not needed until your baby can start crawling around. But if you felt like getting it done early, now is a good time.

Week 32: The Six Week Myth: Dad Edition

This myth is about taking time off from work. I was a victim of this, so mind these words well, because this is a powerful myth. There is a myth that dads either don't get to or shouldn't take any time off to be with their newborn. I believed this fully and never looked into it. My child was maybe two months old when I learned that in California, dads could take a total of six weeks off for Family Bonding Time in the 12 months after a birth. Even when I learned about it, I still felt this social pressure holding me back from considering it. So I didn't. I used the rest of my vacation to take two weeks off after she was born. I paid a stiff penalty for keeping my man-card: I didn't have any more vacation to take when I got sick and I went back to work when I still wasn't sleeping for stretches longer than two hours. So please do consider taking a longer leave if your state and/or job allows for it. If I was to have taken a longer paternity leave, I would have had to start planning months in advance to get coverage. Maybe you have a job like that too, so you'll need to plan ahead. If you do, have a discussion with your partner. Couples do this all sorts of ways. Maybe she'll take her leave time and then you can take yours. Knowing that you're home with the baby might help your partner transition back to work more easily. Plus, if you took six weeks off, this would mean your child would be several months old before going into some other form of care. Even if your partner is staying home with the baby, please consider taking time off to join her in the early weeks and months of this newborn's life!

Preparation Tip: Time to set up the crib and other nursery furniture. Why not invite a parent or a friend with parenting experience over to help?

Week 33: Birthing and Baby Classes

Somewhere in the 2nd to early 3rd trimester, you may sign up for birth, baby care, breastfeeding, infant CPR, and other classes. In the classes that my partner and I attended, I was delighted to see all the dads were present with their partner. The only exception was breastfeeding, in which I was one of only two guys there. On the one hand, based on the content of the video we watched, I guess it's expected for men to miss it. But on the other hand, breastfeeding is an ongoing challenge for your partner to take on and if you attend this you'll be able to support her through whatever happens. By attending the class with my partner, I was able to learn the various positions for baby to be in and what makes a good latch. And as the other guy who attended the class told me during the break, he was happy to learn about breastfeeding because he has felt so helpless during most of the pregnancy and did not want to feel that way after the baby was born.

The birth class had the highest percentage of dads in it and I was glad that we were able to be pretty honest with each other. The emotions of the dads ranged from excited to anxious to terrified to had no idea to "I'm in shock because we just sold the sports car."

Preparation Tip: Install the carseat early so that you're not caught without it if the baby comes early (Thanks to my brother for setting it up at the hospital for us after our baby arrived early!). This also would give you time to visit someplace offering to check to make sure you installed it correctly, something that many places offer. Don't be ashamed; I've heard the percentage of incorrectly installed carseats on the road is astronomical.

Week 34: Go Bag

What do you need in your go-bag for the hospital? Where will you store it while you wait for the magic moment to rush to the hospital? You'll want to be ready to support your partner, so the following is a list of items to consider packing for yourself. Your partner will find a hundred different wonderful lists for expecting mothers, but if you pack your own bag and take responsibility for some of the things on this list, she'll be quite pleased. Try to have it packed early. When we were surprised at Week 37, we only had about 40% of our bag packed.

- Extra batteries for accessories and cell phone chargers
- Backup battery unit that you can plug your cell phone or cell phone charger into (some maternity rooms don't allow you plug anything into their wall sockets)
- Tablet and charging cord
- Video camera (a great item to have to get the best video of the birth, since the lighting is usually not optimal for the average cell phone to take and there will be lots of video you'll want to take)
- Magazines, books, crosswords, etc
- Snacks for yourself to prevent fainting and keep your strength up
- Nothing noxious that your partner won't want to smell
- Two to three extra sets of comfortable clothes, including a special shirt you want to be wearing when you're holding your child for the first time if you have one
- Toothbrush, toothpaste, shaver, deodorant, etc
- Copies of your medical card and birth plan
- Backpack to pack up everything you get while you're there

- Baby name books if the choice is still up in the air
- Fun thank you gifts or small gift cards for the nurses and doctor
- List of who you'll call when you're in labor and another for after the baby is born
- Some dads wear the same shirt to the birth of each of their children. If this is an idea you like, get it packed for this birth and then don't lose it.

Week 35: Super Dad

Don't get rescued. By that, I mean, you'll need to have patience and give yourself plenty of time to figure out how to soothe your baby. Don't allow yourself to give up too quickly (i.e., you give your baby to your partner for her to soothe) or get rescued (i.e., your partner takes the baby before you can figure out how to soothe her or him). Before I go on, let me first declare the difference between what I just described and tag-teaming. I think it's a valuable tool to support each other when your child is fussing by taking turns trying to soothe when the other's methods aren't working or someone's patience is running out. The difference between that and getting rescued is that rescuing happens all the time and stops one partner's chance to try to learn what to do. So, instead of being rescued and never learning how to soothe your child, take the time to figure out which cry means your child needs to be changed, which cry means hunger, and what each other cry means. You'll also need to stay patient, use trial and error, and figure out what strategies soothe your child in what situations. So does your child need to be swaddled, held, rocked, or put in a swing? You'll never feel like more of a competent parent than when you can adequately respond to your child's needs on your own. Both the process of going through this and the competence you feel can help you stay involved through future parenting challenges.

Preparation Tip: Setup to record interesting TV shows and movies and make sure you're subscribed to enough streaming services. You never knew it before, but if you end up pulling all nighters holding your child so she can sleep you will discover that each streaming service only has a finite number of good shows on them!

Week 36: Racing for Pinks (or Blue or Yellow)

Men generally like to be useful and have a concrete impact on whatever we do. So there's a perception that, in situations where our impact is not measurable, we must do all that we can do to be helpful when the time comes. For many men, they believe they have two duties in pregnancy: conception and a speed-demon race-car drive on NOx to the hospital once contractions start. I believe part of the adrenaline that starts pumping when you hear labor is starting is in part built-up energy you've been storing for all the months of not being physically part of the pregnancy. When the moment you've been waiting for arrives, take a moment to relax and think back over the whole pregnancy. Take a moment to think about how you have gone beyond what society has taught men to do during pregnancy. Remember how you've used these months to connect more to your partner, to get involved in the pregnancy, and to support the mother of your child through all the changes she has been experiencing. Take pride in how much impact you have had on this journey already. Then take a deep breath and follow the hospital plan and enjoy all that this miraculous experience has to offer. For me, when my wife said she thought her water broke, I was just finishing up in the bathroom. I was shocked (partially because our little one was three weeks early) and so I had to ask myself, "Do I wash my hands first or run to her?!" Then logic took over, I washed my hands, and I got to show off that I'd remembered from birth class about what specific information the doctor would want to know when we called. And remember, you'll want to drive safely to the hospital but you're gonna have to fight against adrenaline and emotions to do it.

Preparation Tip: Is there such a thing as banking enough sleep to last you for the next few years? If you found a way to do it, starting trying now!

Week 37: Coach?

What kind of a coach will you be for your partner? It is interesting that this role, supporting your partner through the birth of your child, is called a coach. As men, who do we think of when we think of coaches? Most men think of the great strategy-geniuses, the play-calling wizards, and the charismatic leaders of our favorite sports teams. Sports coaches forge the direction of an endeavor and create the vision of the team. Be careful not to take this version of coach to your role during labor and delivery. You need to focus on your partner and anticipate her needs. You probably won't be calling the plays here; you'll read the situation and respond with what you think she'd want most. But to do this, you'll need to memorize the play book. The choices during birth are more numerous than any first-timer might imagine so be sure to talk together about the decisions you both prefer. Some choices will be easy while other choices will be preferences you decide in the moment. By talking through these decisions together, you'll be able to confidently communicate with the birth staff what your partner wants. If you don't take the time before labor to get to know what she wants, then you won't be able to assist in making decisions during labor. Therefore, I'll propose advocate, partner, and supporter being better labels for your role than coach. Advocate for her needs and for the birth plan that you both created; support her with massages, back rubs, and ice chips; and partner with her to share the responsibilities in the journey toward taking your first family selfie!

Preparation Tip: My sister-in-law swears by drinking cherry juice for new moms to help in the recovery process so maybe you'll want to have a bottle ready to go in the fridge for your partner when you get home. Even if it doesn't really work or your partner thinks it's silly, I imagine this winning you lots of brownie points for having been proactive for her recovery. The recovery for the mom is something no one ever talks about enough as the focus is usually on the pregnancy and birthing process.

Week 38: Doula, midwife, mother, doctor, nurses...

Have you and your partner discussed where you fit in during labor and delivery? There could be a room full of nurses, doctors, midwives, a doula, and other family members. What roles do you want and not want during the birth of your child? It's important you feel comfortable in your role, because the more comfortable you feel, the better you'll be able to comfort and support your partner through her experience. Do you want to be very active in the birth? Do you know how active your partner wants you? Will you be stationed by her head, will you be assisting her to push by holding her leg, or will you be "catching" your baby and assisting in the actual delivery? It is important to know what roles you want and don't want to have, as once the process starts, there will be a lot going on and a lot of new faces buzzing around you. All the professionals in the room will be doing tasks they do daily and taking care of a wide variety of responsibilities and roles, so they won't have time to help you decide what your role will be. Plus, since the professional staff does this job daily, you may be facing the assumption that dads don't want to be too involved. You never know what experiences they will have had with men before, so don't leave what you'll experience up to anyone but yourself and your partner by being assertive, clear, and sure. So, as you and your partner review all the birth plan choices you'll make to customize this experience, be sure to discuss thoroughly how you enter into the equation so that when the moment comes, you'll both be able to immediately vocalize what you'll be doing.

Week 39: Cord Cutter

For me, cutting the umbilical cord was quite an experience and I remember having no idea what it would be like. Cutting it felt kinda like cutting an uncooked chicken breast and I was not expecting that so it took a few snips for my first kid. I got a drop of blood on my pants from cutting the cord, which was a reminder that this ritual was literally cutting off my daughter's way of living for the past 37 weeks and helping her transition to living more independently. It was a moment that felt like a promise to our child, that we would raise her to be strong and independent. As the nurses did a flurry of tests and measures on our child, I felt extremely excited and extremely scared to hold her. Watching their deftness at holding her, diapering her, examining her, and whatever else they did so quickly, I worried about dropping her when they gave her to me. These fears were surprises to me, because I had felt very confident about this part since I had taken care of my nephew when he was a newborn and toddler. I had been afraid of birth because nothing really felt like it could prepare me for such an event, no matter what I read, and I thought the taking care of a newborn would be more doable in comparison. But when they put my daughter in my arms, I instantly knew I could do whatever it would mean to raise her and I was grateful to my wife for going through pregnancy and birth to bring this little miracle out and into our lives.

Week 40: Epilogue

Depending on how your labor story went, how much sleep you lost during the birth process, and depending on how much your newborn sleeps, you may be the most sleepy you've ever been in your life during your one to three days in the hospital. For us, the water broke at around 10 at night and our daughter was born around dinner time the next day, so we were both exhausted. Luckily, we had talked about a long, overnight labor and so I knew that once she had the epidural, my job was to get as much sleep as possible so that I'd be ready to take over once the baby was born and she could get some sleep to start recovering. So I did my best to sleep on the hard couch that turns into something like a bed for dads. This was especially important because my wife didn't sleep much at all since they had to check her vital signs and everything else every few hours throughout the labor. So as my wife slept, I sleepily watched as my baby fussed and cried through first pictures, the hearing test, and other things I can't remember. We enjoyed our hospital time, as the nurses did all the work, and we took our time getting the press release out onto social media so that we could have some time for just family and rest before everyone else would stop by. My mother-in-law knew that her job was to bring a pizza from my wife's favorite place, so we ate like royalty. Just before we went home, we got to press a button and the whole hospital played a nursery rhyme to announce our new baby. This was a tearful moment because we had seen this done during our hospital tour months ago but could never imagine that it would actually happen and we'd be bringing home a new life. As we drove home, it was quite a stark contrast to driving to the hospital.

Everything seemed brighter, cars seemed to drive faster and scarier, and I drove slower, compared to the excited, heart-pounding race to the hospital on the way in. We took video as we brought our little one into our home, showed her around, introduced her to the cats, and then placed her in the bassinet as she slept. This would be the only time she slept in the bassinet because she was a tough one to get asleep, but it was nice to get video of it because I had slept in that same bassinet. Having her sleeping in the nursery, it brought home all that we had done to prepare our lives and home for this new person. I looked at all the furniture we'd bought and all the baby shower gifts that now had meaning. My dad had come over and we'd built the crib together with parenthood on the horizon for me, and so I felt a sense of family and friends all around me. I look forward to these moments for you and I hope you have a healthy and safe pregnancy and birth experience that pops out a healthy little human. I wrote this book mainly in 2010 during our first pregnancy and then in 2011 during the birth and new baby experiences. Once my little one started crawling around, I got too busy and tired for the next nine years but I finally started to edit it once she and my son were both in school. I'm happy to say that society's stark gender roles have eased a bit more since then, and I truly believe this book will be obsolete within my lifetime.

Appendices

What follows from here are a few longer chapters about life with a newborn. I found whole new space and cognition in my mind while trying to get my daughter to sleep at night so I report on my brilliant thoughts at 3 am. Then I was a Mommy in a Mommy's Group and I smuggled back what I learned for the first year of my daughter's life. I also poke fun at all the new words and information you have to learn as new parents and include my chart to help you figure out how to buy baby clothes. I end with a short explanation about the secret meaning of the title of the book.

(This page from Oh, the Daddy You'll Be! welcomes you to the Parenting Club!)

You'll learn to hold newborns.

You'll track your kid's bowels!

You'll join those called parents who talk more in vowels.

Appendix I: What I Learned at 3 am!

There were many sleepless nights as a new father, and I discovered many things about the life I was beginning and some things about life I had never noticed:

Don't cry over spilled milk doesn't apply to breast milk, especially when your baby is going through a growth spurt and every drop is needed to prevent a meltdown!

Reading "A Tale of Two Cities" to your newborn might not be proven to make her smarter, but it sure does put her to sleep! (Just read the beheading parts to yourself)

Late night TV and commercials are as bad as they say

We used these new types of bottles that came with several pieces inside the bottle to help prevent colic. Late one night, while washing the hundreds of pieces for the millionth time, I started fantasizing about inviting other new dads to come over to play poker and using our collective stockpile of bottle pieces as poker chips.

Now I get it: getting up 4 to 8 times a night with your baby teaches you how not to need sleep and how to get up at the drop of a pacifier. That is how our parents learned how to detect us coming home late after curfew or sneaking down stairs for some late night ice cream, hearing just the slightest creak in a floorboard. As infants, we gave them the skills to catch us in the act sixteen years later. Karma's a beach.

As you can see from the example above, I started to speak a foreign language. After your child is born, I think something genetic takes place that switches out swear words in your brain with new replacements. Just be sure, as you go to work on three hours of sleep, that you don't start saying "Stinky Poopee Pants" and "Gosh Goobers" at the water cooler. Of course, the other parents in the circle will nod understandingly as the rest laugh at you.

Just because my partner started cheering for every burp and fart our baby does, that doesn't mean she'll cheer for mine too.

Did you know you can burp yourself through your baby? I was amazed at how many times I had my baby over my shoulder while burping her, and all the sudden I burped. This got to be a bit comical when around family who were hoping to hear my baby burp (cause they knew it would make her feel better and end the fussiness). I would eventually "burp myself" and they would cheer, thinking I had gotten a burp from her.

Batteries are to baby devices (bouncer, jumper, etc) as print cartridges are to printers, since both examples are expensive things you have to replace often. The only difference is that at least printer companies have the decency to sell the printers for cheap, while both the devices and the constantly changed batteries are expensive in the baby world. We got around the cost a little by buying rechargeable batteries; the only downside is that you have to replace those more often. Therefore, an important tip is to keep a few small sized Phillips and flathead screwdrivers around to open the battery compartments.

Having hiccups at the same time as your baby may seem like a precious moment, but just wait till you get her to sleep and your next hiccup wakes her back up again!

Appendix II: What I Learned in Deep Undercover at a Mommies Group

The Six Week Myth: Chores Edition. Most women take at least six weeks off work for their maternity leave. During that time, the dads get used to her doing everything and so adjusting can be hard when she goes back to work. It sets up the relationship for the Second Shift phenomenon, where mom's go back to work all day but still come home to the second shift of childcare, cooking, and cleaning. Watch out for this. Now many women said they needed to be more active with these activities while they were home on leave because they would go crazy if they didn't have these familiar things to do. So, it's not necessarily a bad thing. Just don't somehow forget how to do laundry and all the other duties on your half of the list. Believe me, the biggest swear word in a group of moms, second only to "my-baby-is-sick," is "second shift." They spit that word out like venom and you don't want to be the recipient of such group-hate.

The Other Six Week Myth: Riding the Bench Edition. Most OB-GYN's will check your partner at about six weeks and verify that she's healing okay. Of course, all you'll be focusing on is one particular purpose of the appointment: can sexual activity start again?! The idea that six weeks is enough time for a woman to heal, and the idea that her doctor can magically decide when it won't hurt anymore for her to have sex, are both myths. Besides the physical healing that needs to happen, women have to feel ready. I don't even want to think of a metaphor of birthing a baby that would apply to men so that we could have more empathy for our partners desire to get back in the saddle slowly. But a lot of men I talked to were impatient about the restarting of their love lives and a lot of women I talked to said it hurt when their partner's convinced them to start back up earlier than they wanted.

Work and Parenting Intersection: A major moment for conflict is when one partner's been at home with baby all day and then the other comes home. Many miscommunications can happen here (in this example, the dad has gone to work and the mom is home today, but as we know any of these characters can be any gender). Mom worries he's been stressing all day at work and doesn't need the stress of baby when he comes home. Dad stresses over taking baby from mom because he doesn't want to disturb the mom/child relationship and peace he is seeing when he gets home. Mom really wants dad to take baby right when he gets home and gets mad at dad for not thinking of how hard she's worked all day. Dad just wants a little break when he gets home before moving in to try to figure out babycare, something that might seem harder to him than his job (because at work you get feedback, training, causality, tech support, and breaks.). Mom worries about giving baby to dad because he doesn't try to reinforce the same schedule, cues, routines, or other aspects of baby care that she's been working on all day, and dad worries about taking baby because he feels like he will get judged for doing it wrong or he worries he will do it wrong and mess up the baby before its time for sleep, etc. So the solution for all these worries: talk it out and figure out your solution. One couple had dad stay in the car for a half hour after he got home and read a book, so that he could take the break he wanted from work while still remotely available if needed, and then he was better prepared to come in and take baby off of mom's hands.

Mother's Day: This is very important to most women as it's their first Mother's Day, and most men fail at it (including me, because I was too tired, too busy with new baby duties, and didn't plan ahead. I didn't even get my card written and I spent three hours shopping the day before and left mom with baby, and never found what she asked for, so I had to leave on Mother's Day to get her gift and took baby, so she could sleep, which was a win). Best idea to succeed at Mother's Day: plan ahead! If you put as much effort into Mother's Day as you do planning a Super Bowl party, you'll win husband of the decade, because most of us men fail at this! Just keep it simple though: ask her what would make a great Mother's Day. Some new moms want a day away from baby so they could go out with their friends and get a taste of their old life. Other new moms though would be horrified by such an idea (because they don't want to be away from baby, because they have to feed baby and haven't gotten the hang of pumping yet, etc.) and would rather have a simple day at home or at a picnic where maybe you and other family do even more of the baby care. So don't forget to ask what she actually wants with enough time to pull it off!

Assumptions: As the only dad in this group, I became the go-to person for complaints about some of the ladies' husbands. One woman complained that her husband took forever to feed their baby at night. She normally breastfed, so for her, she had a supply on-demand. But he took his time warming the bottle just right, changed the diaper, and then got their child comfortable just-so, before finally feeding her so they could get back to sleep. She wanted him to, instead, just use a bottle that she pumped at the beginning of the night so he could feed her on-demand and return to sleep in minutes. I of course offered all sorts of suggestions, and we all joked that maybe he was trying to get out of this late night feeding duty by doing a bad job. But I also just simply told her to just ask what his motives were. Turned out that he was so tired of being away from his child all day (and being exhausted when he came home from work), that he felt he wanted to spoil his child at 4 am and do this feeding as lovingly as possible. We all learned a great lesson about making assumptions by this.

Instructions: Best quote from a mom, about guys putting together all the toys and devices for the new baby: "Guys should know that we read the directions just enough so that we can tell them when they're doing it wrong!"

Don't Compare Babies: A critical lesson: keep yourself, your partner, and your relationship sane by promising to not compare your baby to other babies you know, read about, or are told about by others. Every baby is different. I can't tell you how many times this came up: sleep schedules, sleep locations, feeding, abilities (how early your baby can turn over, for example), etc. Each baby varies on so many different continuums that it is not helpful to try to compare or learn totally from other examples. My assumption is that you'll get plenty of others telling you what to do. They do it out of love for you (or maybe because they see you're a first-timer and a dad, which they may see as two strikes against you), but don't forget that you're the one who knows your particular baby the best.

Surprisingly Wonderful: I just wanted to admit here,

before going on my soapbox in the next section, that I was really unsure about attending the mommies group. It was hard to imagine that I'd enjoy it and I didn't really want to make new friends. I didn't see the point in meeting a bunch of other new parents. My friends like babies too, some even had some, so why do we need new friends? Well, I went and enjoyed it, and I also found that I really valued these new friendships with new parents a lot too. There is something completely different and completely comforting about getting to know people going through almost exactly the same life change as you are. After getting to know these new moms, and later meeting their partners, I was very proud that I had had the courage to be open to new experiences and new friends. It was the shared newness among new friends that helped us get through the sleepless nights, the scary moments, the "What the heck is the right choice?" moments, and the poop stories. As a new parent these days, there is so much different advice, different scary stories and warnings on the internet, and differing opinions from pediatricians, that you need to be in a group of friends of kids almost the same age as yours to really understand what your micro-generation of parents is going through. We remain great friends with some of those families still!

Secret Knowledge: The biggest discovery I made while attending the mommies group was that groups like this is where moms get their secret knowledge. Many men would never get caught dead in a mommies group, yet what they don't know is that this is where their partners are getting all that good baby knowledge. Basically, I discovered why so many men feel like they're never going to be as good a parent as their partners. What these men don't know is that women go to baby basic training and learn all sorts of knowledge. Not only do they learn about a weekly topic that ranges from "How to Calm Your Crying Baby" to "Babies and Sleep" to "Strategies to Raise a Healthy Child," they also learn the skills of parenting in a supportive environment. They get to bring the baby to a room full of moms (and hopefully a few dads or more) and practice calming, putting to sleep, changing a diaper, and feeding your baby. Sound like no big deal? Just wait till your first diaper change in public. Especially your first diaper change in front of a bunch of moms. Something you perfected when your child was three days old has now regressed back to "bumbling, fumbling, how'd that poop get there?" status. And how does your partner stay so calm as your baby fusses and cries out in public? It's because she's held conversations with a room full of people, all while your baby or three others are crying. Believe me, this social practice helps. So at least give it a fraction of a second of thought. If you, like almost every man, just can't see yourself there (remember, I couldn't see myself there either), then see if you and the other dads of newborns that you know can get together and BBQ or take a hike or something that gives you the same learning environment. And remember to ask your partner to bring home the handouts and talk to you about what she learned in her mommies group, because then you'll be in on the secret knowledge too.

Postpartum Emotions and Men: I would like to seriously and sincerely mention that dads get baby blues and post-partum depression too. So much so that there are now resources for men, like hotlines, support groups, and web pages (PostPartumMen.com is one example). So, don't become some self-sacrificing man who needs to be the protector of his mate and fails to take care of himself. Having your own supports, routines, and breaks from baby care are important for your mental health. Finding other dads to talk to or meet up with somewhat regularly might be the best thing you do for your child. Why's that? Because the more stable and healthy you are, the better job you will be able to do taking care of your child.

Postpartum Emotions and Your Partner: Baby blues and postpartum depression happen to lots of women. Baby blues and postpartum depression are completely normal aspects of this process for some new moms. Baby blues and postpartum depression make up a whole area of psychology and many psychologists, psychiatrists, counseling centers, health centers, and other helpers focus just on this very normal part of having a child. As I said before, it is likely that baby blues and postpartum depression will not feel like some "disease" or something foreign to your partner's everyday experiences. They are very good at going undetected and doing their dirty work. You, as her partner, can play a large role in identifying that something is happening outside of your normal experience of her. Please, don't take that as a privilege to tell your partner, "You're so emotional now, I'm not listening to you; you're just having postpartum depression." Instead, suggest to her that you are concerned about her and want her to think about whether or not these very normal and common experiences are happening to her.

Postpartum Adjustment: Grief. With every good change in life usually comes grief for what has been lost. Even if you were planning for this birth for years and years or if it was a surprise, don't be surprised if you feel some loss for what was. A wonderful college professor teaching Life Span Development stated that on one bleary-eyed night when his baby again wouldn't sleep, he went through the dictionary whiting out words that no longer applied to him, like Spontaneous, Competent, and Well-Rested.

Postpartum Adjustment: Snapping Turtles. Even if you and your partner are the master of the respectful fight, with perfect decorum and charm, your skills of respectful disagreements will be tested. So try to remember to have empathy when fights go a bit too far.

Postpartum Adjustment: Stay United. Now that you have a child, you and your partner may be spending more time together but it is time where you're distracted or taking turns with the baby or napping at odd hours. You will have all new pressures on your relationship, like people dropping by unannounced or you making plans and forgetting to tell your partner. You may make assumptions, like telling one set of grandparents that of course your baby will wear the outfit they made for a special day, and this may cause rifts you didn't foresee. Rule of thumb, take it slow, check in with each other, and try to talk through how the major milestones will go and make new plans for how decisions and schedules will be made. These are topics you actually figured out as a new couple when you first met, whether you talked about them or not, and now you'll have to figure it out all over again.

Postpartum Adjustment: Priorities and Ideals. Your relationship had found its own status quo a long time ago about what you believed in, what kind of foods you eat, and how you prioritize your money, but parenthood brings whole new challenges to that status quo. You and your partner will need to decide how much you care about Organic and Natural and Non-GMO and When to start screen time and How much screen time and What kind of parenting to use and How to sleep train and How important is a structured schedule, etc etc etc. Just like when the election of an unexpected President rips apart couples who suddenly find out how deeply different they are, these challenges can rip you apart if you let them. Figure out what matters most to you and find ways to compromise. Remember that humans have raised babies in thousands of ways and today's society offers thousands of options and still most people end up okay.

Dads Returning to Work: Dads generally return to work before their partners, as I did, so I write this section with that stereotype in mind. What is it like returning to work? From my experience and others I spoke with, it's generally a multifaceted experience. On the one side, it is hard to leave our newborn baby and partner, especially in the early weeks when you both are still trying to figure out how to be parents, how to soothe your child, and trying to figure out answers to a million other questions. On the other hand, being a new dad is a new challenge, one where there are plenty of moments where you may lack confidence in your abilities. So returning to work, where you know what you're doing and where you receive concrete feedback, can be a calming experience. But you add in the lack of sleep and you may not find yourself working at peak performance. So how do you plan your return to work, in light of all this? One suggestion is to return to work midweek, so you do not have to put in a full work week for your first week. Second, make sure to talk to your partner about who will handle what chores around the house and who will make meals. Be sure to be open to what will work in this new life, not just what worked before your baby was born.

Tips to be a Supportive Partner: If your partner is pumping, especially if she is exclusively pumping, there are lots of ways to be supportive. Just imagine having to hook yourself up to that contraption six to eight times a day (sometimes a lot more often in the beginning) and you'll quickly see that this is an easy area to support your partner. First of all, she has to wash her equipment after each pumping, and this is an easy place to jump in and take over (I recommend buying a second set of the accessories. It cuts down on how often you have to wash them, plus provides a backup if a piece malfunctions). Second, if she's pumping, there's a good chance she's trying to store some up for the future, and you can take over as Milk Inventory Manager. This includes FIFO'ing (First In, First Out) the milk so that when you defrost the milk later, you're using the oldest milk first (check with your doctor about how long breast milk can last at room temperature, while refrigerated, and when frozen: you'll find a maddening variation of answers to these questions online and between you and your friends, so I say just go with what your doctor says!). One tip to make FIFO'ing easier: use different brand milk storage bags each month, so that all the bags from one month are easy to recognize. By being a part of the breast milk process in these ways, your partner will love you more (not guaranteed) and you will feel more a part of the process that is feeding your child.

Appendix III: An Irreverent Reference List

Poop: A word that will enter in your everyday conversations even more than it did when you were four years old

Diaper Can: What you'll rename your trash can, since they will make up so much of what you throw in there

Reusable Diapers: Mother Nature's cruel way to make you reaffirm your dedication to her survival one dirty diaper at a time

Diaper Sprayer: Warning: the first few rows will get sprayed. While your hands won't touch as much poop if you use one of these, don't believe the hype that you'll never have to touch poopy water. You'll be setting yourself up for gross disappointment.

Diaper Bag: Consider it your baby briefcase and wear it proudly

Laundry Tab: No, this is not the bill you'll get from that fancy diaper service you've contracted with so that you didn't have to spray poopy diapers or touch poop. And no, this is not the money you'll get paid for doubling the amount of laundry you do in a week now.

Diaper Service: Modern day miracle workers, you leave them dirty diapers on your doorstep and they leave you clean ones. If only they would come in the house and change the diapers too...

Butt Paste™: The most hysterically named gift we received at our baby shower, with second place going to BumGenius™

Newborn Size Clothes: Really small clothes that only fit the newest of newborns. AKA, the clothes that will look the newest and make the best hand-me-downs to your next child since your newborn will only be able to wear them for such a short period of time. But since you won't be sleeping too much during this time and you'll be changing diapers around 10 to 12 times a day, you'll see them more often and may still feel like you've gotten your money's worth.

Layette: This word was specifically invented to confuse those brave men who try to master shopping for baby clothes

Hospital Bill: An amazing mathematical equation that defies the laws of logic to deliver you the highest bill possible

Hiccups: Pre-historic baby-finder-system

Baby Teeth: The natural predator of first the sleeping baby and then the nursing woman

Pets: Little furry things you used to love as if they were your babies

Mommies Groups: Contrary to popular belief, babies are allowed at these groups too

Formula: Expensive

Bouncer: A vibrating chair that bounces. Yes, you will fantasize about getting an adult sized one to sit in while playing video games. Many parents found that this chair gave them their only chance at taking a shower or visiting the toilet.

Gym: Usually a mat for babies to lie on while looking up at hanging things they swat at. No monthly membership fees really set babies up for disappointment later on in life.

Jumper: Resist the temptation to call this your babysitter

Baby Food: The reason our brains are not able to

remember our first few years of life

Bottle: Now when you say you're going to go hit the bottle, it's code for washing the day's bottles and all their little pieces

Nipple Flow: A reason to make you buy more nipples every couple of months

Baby Sneezes: Look just like adult sneezes, except babies can't seem to master the cover your nose part

Baby Hats: Things that you're told a million times how important they are for babies to wear, which is why you put them back on her a million times when they keep falling off. Also, a pointy knit hat is the best way to make your baby look like a garden gnome

Baby Socks: See Baby Hats

Vaccinations: Rule of thumb, take a vacation day on vaccination day, as your baby will take all day to vehemently remind you that they hate vaccines

Pediatrician: Be careful on your tone and inflection when calling them Baby Doctors

Hospital Stay: No, the nurses won't come to your house to change your baby's diapers there, so don't get used to it

Perry Bottle: A crucial mobile bidet

Baby Eye Color: Will they change or stay the same? You'll spend six months staring into your baby's eyes asking this question; while your baby will be staring back saying, I hope mine don't look like his.

Baby Features: Sometimes they look like Mommy, sometimes they look like Daddy, sometimes they look like the letter carrier. Try not to rush to conclusions (at least go on Maury first).

Designer Baby Clothes: Don't swear you'll never buy these, cause it hurts when your pants are on fire

Poop: Something that makes you seriously consider throwing out whatever it touches

Receiving Blanket: Apparently, not just for receiving. (and not the cloth that receivers wear to dry their hands between plays)

Nap Time: A finite period of time you'll spend most of paralyzed wondering how to spend it best

Swaddling: The fine art of turning babies into burritos

Sleep Sacks: Fart collector. AKA Instant Mermaid AKA Instant Potato Sack Racer AKA Baby in a pillow case (do not place babies in pillow cases)

Gown: A parent's godsend when it's diaper changing time

Family Bed: Ironically, in Latin this translates to, "No more new additions to the family for a while"

Baby Proofed: Practice, practice, practice: you'll never live it down if you can't open a baby-proofed drawer

Baby Proofing: The art of crawling on one's hands and knees, looking for possible dangers that could hurt your baby. Also known as, "Oh Crap, They Can Crawl Day."

Colic: The biggest four-letter word in the newborn world

Sleep: Something that babies do and adults daydream of

College Fund: the estimates of what will be needed down the road are larger than the value of your house

Pacifier: The true Easy Button™

Days: Long

Years: Short

Love: The easiest thing to give, and the thing babies need the most of

Happiness: A baby's smile

(Did you notice I included poop twice? That's because it gets everywhere.)

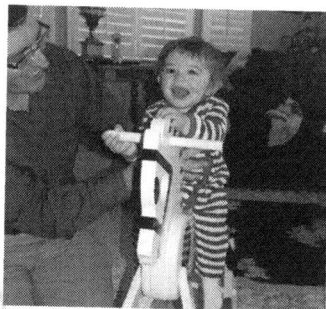

Appendix IV: Baby Clothes Cheat Sheet

	Jan	Feb	Mar	Apr	May
Newborn 0-6 week	Wi	Wi	Wi/Sp	Sp	Sp/Su
0-3 Months (aka 3 Mo)	Wi/Sp	Wi/Sp	Sp	Sp/Su	Su
0-6 Months	Sp/Su	Sp/Su	Sp/Su	Su/Fa	Su/Fa
3-6 Months (aka 6 Mo)	Sp/Su	Su	Su	Su/Fa	Su/Fa
3-9 Months	Su/Fa	Su/Fa	Su/Fa	Fa/Wi	Fa/Wi
6-9 Months	Su/Fa	Su/Fa	Fa	Fa/Wi	Fa/Wi
6-12 Months	Fa/Wi	Fa/Wi	Fa/Wi	Wi/Spi	Wi/Sp
12 Months 9-12	Wi	Wi	Wi	Wi/Sp	Wi/Sp
18 Months	Sp/Su	Sp/Su	Sp/Su	Su/Fa	Su/Fa
24 Months	Fa/Wi	Fa/Wi	Fa/Wi	Wi/Sp	Wi/Sp
2T	Fa/Wi	Wi	Wi/Sp	Wi/Sp	Sp

Wi=Winter, Sp=Spring, Su=Summer, Fa=Fall

Find your child's birth month or the month of their due date along the top. Use that column to determine approximately what season your baby will be in for each clothing size. See Week 22: Baby Clothes Cheat Sheet for more information

Jun	Jul	Aug	Sep	Oct	Nov	Dec
Su	Su	Su/Fa	Fa	Fa/Wi	Wi	Wi
Su	Su/Fa	Su/Fa	Fa/Wi	Wi	Wi	Wi
Su/Fa	Fa/Wi	Fa/Wi	Fa/Wi	Wi/Sp	Wi/Sp	Wi/Sp
Fa	Fa	Fa/Wi	Wi	Wi	Wi/Sp	Wi/Sp
Fa/Wi	Wi/Sp	Wi/Sp	Wi/Sp	Sp/Su	Sp/Su	Sp/Su
Wi	Wi/Sp	Wi/Sp	Wi/Sp	Sp/Su	Sp/Su	Su
W/ Sp	Sp/Su	Sp/Su	Sp/Su	Su/Fa	Su/Fa	Su/Fa
Sp	Sp/Su	Su	Su	Su/Fa	Fa	Fa/Wi
Su/Fa	Fa/Wi	Fa/Wi	Fa/Wi	Wi/Sp	Wi/Sp	Wi/Sp
Wi/Sp	Sp/Su	Sp/Su	Sp/Su	Su/Fa	Su/Fa	Su/Fa
Sp/Su	Sp/Su	Su	Su/Fa	Su/Fa	Fa	Fa/Wi

Secret Chapter about the Secret Meaning of the Title

Fatherhood Begins Before Birth has a secret meaning. Of course, the title is primarily a call to men to live up to the challenge to start their development into great fathers and co-parenting partners during pregnancy. But my hope is that we raise the next generation of children in a manner that helps them grow to become naturally great fathers. If we can continue to instill qualities of great fathers in our boys as we raise them, the need for this book will vanish.

Made in the USA
Las Vegas, NV
19 November 2020